# YOUR KNOWLEDGE HAS VALUE

AF143527

- We will publish your bachelor's and master's thesis, essays and papers

- Your own eBook and book - sold worldwide in all relevant shops

- Earn money with each sale

## Upload your text at www.GRIN.com and publish for free

**Bibliographic information published by the German National Library:**

The German National Library lists this publication in the National Bibliography; detailed bibliographic data are available on the Internet at http://dnb.dnb.de .

**Imprint:**

Copyright © 2019 GRIN Verlag
Print and binding: Books on Demand GmbH, Norderstedt Germany
ISBN: 9783346017284

**This book at GRIN:**

https://www.grin.com/document/497313

Gabriel Kabanda

# Review of Human Computer Interaction and Computer Vision

GRIN Verlag

**GRIN - Your knowledge has value**

Since its foundation in 1998, GRIN has specialized in publishing academic texts by students, college teachers and other academics as e-book and printed book. The website www.grin.com is an ideal platform for presenting term papers, final papers, scientific essays, dissertations and specialist books.

**Visit us on the internet:**

http://www.grin.com/

http://www.facebook.com/grincom

http://www.twitter.com/grin_com

# REVIEW OF HUMAN COMPUTER INTERACTION AND COMPUTER VISION

**Gabriel Kabanda**

Atlantic International University

## ABSTRACT

The review below describes or analyses the trends and best practices in Human Computer Interaction and Computer Vision. Human-Computer Interaction (HCI) is a computer user interface which the user of the system works with to achieve their given tasks and sees the system in use. Information Technology (IT) is essentially an integrated person-machine system that provides information support operations, management and decision-making. Human Computer Interaction (HCI) focuses on the interactions between human and computer systems to achieve the IT system functionality, user experience, usability, the support of user interaction effectiveness. Users are increasingly preferring the use of online business systems and so are becoming intolerant of systems which are not user friendly. The human factor is an attribute (physical or cognitive) which is specific to people that use a system and how it influences the normal operations of the system as well as the achievement of human-environment equilibriums. Surface technology eliminates input/output devices through a touch sensitive feature which plays the role of input/output devices as a result of the merger between the physical and the virtual world. Through surface technology, the user eliminates the use of GUI mediums and reduces the gap between the physical and the virtual world.There are two classes of surface technology, one for the display and the other one which uses a touch sensitive mechanism for the interpretation of user signals. New approaches and methods are now needed in HCI to equip researchers with a better understanding of designing interactive systems. There are new interactive possibilities to be explored in audio-based mobile technology. The increasing popularity of smartphones has proved the portability, adaptability and 'always on' capability of geo-locative interactive systems. HCI bridges the gap between humans and computing devices with respect to observation of interactions, analysis of the involved interactions and the the human consequences of the interaction. The focus of HCI is the practice of usability which includes look-and-feel features, appeal, utility, efficiency, effectiveness and safety.

**Key Words:** Human computer Interaction (HCI), Computer Vision, Graphical User Interface (GUI), WIMP, voice user interface, surface technology, human factor, usability, functionality.

## Table of Contents

# 1. ANALYTICAL EXPOSITION

The paper presents an analytical exposition, critical context and integrative conclusion on the trends and best practices in Human Computer Interaction and Computer Vision. Human-Computer Interaction (HCI) is a computer user interface which the user of the system works with to achieve their given tasks and sees the system in use. Information Technology (IT) is essentially an integrated person-machine system that provides information support operations, management and decision-making. Human Computer Interaction (HCI) focuses on the interactions between human and computer systems to achieve the IT system functionality, user experience, usability, the support of user interaction effectiveness (Draganova, A, and Doran, P., 2013, p.245). According to Draganova, A., and Doran, P. (2013, p.245), users are increasingly preferring the use of online business systems and so are becoming intolerant of systems which are not user friendly. The field of human-computer interaction has increasingly become more devoted to the processes and context for the user interface.

The object of HCI is to design design computer systems supportive of user productivity and safety. Humans and machines interact through a user interface which facilitates the manipulation and monitoring of the system status. Functionality of a system is defined by the set of actions or services that it provides to its users. Usability of a system describes how a system can be used efficiently and adequately to accomplish a task. An effective design process pays attention to the work being supported and the users that operate the system. The human factor is an attribute (physical or cognitive) which is specific to people that use a system and how it influences the normal operations of the system as well as the achievement of human-environment equilibriums. The three most commonly used user interfaces are:

a) The popular Graphical User Interface (GUI),

b) the Voice User Interface, and

c) the Multi-Modal Interface which uses a combination of several methods of user input into a system.

The user interface can be broadly classified into the command line interface and GUI. The command line interface requires the user to provide an input in the form of a command at the command prompt, for example on UNIX shells. The GUI comprises the Window, Icon, Menus and Pointers (WIMP) and facilitates interaction through graphical elements. However, the GUI is more user friendly and attractive to use than the command line interface. The command, files and folders can be represented by an image called an icon.

Surface technology eliminates input/output devices through a touch sensitive feature which plays the role of input/output devices as a result of the merger between the physical and the virtual world (Farooq, U., *et al*, 2011, p.25). Through surface technology, the user eliminates the use of GUI mediums and reduces the gap between the physical and the virtual world. According to Farooq, U, *et al* (2011, p.26), a user interacts with the digitalized world by just a finger touch by virtue of the surface technology. There are two classes of surface technology, one for the display and the other one which uses a touch sensitive mechanism for the interpretation of user signals. Farooq, U., *et al* (2011, p.26) points out that the display component can be built on the display platform. On the contrary, the user signal interpretation component is based on an image taken by image sensing cameras which are generally infrared based. In such a setup, cameras are adjusted in a manner that covers the whole screen. The three ways in which the infrared based sensing can be achieved are frustrated total internal reflection, diffuse illumination, and diffused surface illumination (Farooq, U., *et al*, 2011, p.26). Straight user communication can be provided by direct interaction with the screen which nullifies the use of input devices such as mouse or a keyboard. In this way multiple processing points are offered simultaneously, which is unlike a mouse that provides only one point where the cursor is being processed, whilst user interaction is being made available at a common time slice. Surface technology brings a complete revolution on how people interact with computers (Farooq, U., *et al*, 2011, p.27). This the technology which is now widely adopted on touch sensitive screens.

HCI adequately addresses the various needs of user groups and individuals. Practical research contributions in HCI reveals unknown insights concerning the degree of interaction between the end user and the technology, called the affordance. HCI is abound with practical research methods such as field experiments, formal experiments, field studies, surveys, focus groups, interviews, usability tests, contextual inquiry, case studies, ethnography, diary studies, automated data collection, and experience sampling (Lopes, A.G., 2016, p.365). HCI, as a multidisciplinary field, draws benefits and contributions from diverse areas such as psychology, organisational and social science, computer science, and cognitive science, with the view to investigate user experience and interaction with technology. A wide range of research methods are used in HCI since this arena is multidisciplinary in nature, and hence the amalgamation **of** research methods commonly used in engineering, the social sciences, and medical fields.

Organisations use various methods and tools to improve the design process of user interfaces and its evaluation, which differs from project to project objectives (Lopes, A.G., 2016, p.367). Active participation of users in the user interface design can be achieved through a user-centred design and the interaction of design and evaluation. The most commonly used user centred design methods include user requirements, field study, evaluation, formal heuristics evaluation, focus groups, user interviews, surveys, prototype without user testing, iterative design, usability task analysis, card sorting, informal expert review, and participatory design (Lopes, A.G., 2016, p.367).

## 2. CRITICAL CONTEXT

Human computer interaction (HCI) is a multi-disciplinary domain that handles the theory, design, implementation, and evaluation of the technical affordance of the computing devices (Kim, G.J., 2015, p.1). The abstract model of the interaction between users and the computing device helps us to understand the nature of interaction, where the interface is a choice of technical realization of such a given interaction model. Commercial success of software products now requires the simple aesthetic appeal of interfaces as a critical element, as has been amply demonstrated by the design of Apple® products. Kim, G.J. (2015, p.2) warned of the difficulty in accomplishing a good design, mainly because it is a multi-objective task that involves simultaneous consideration of diverse elements that include characteristics of the tasks, category of users, capabilities and cost of the devices, exact quantitative evaluation measures, or lack of objective. What is required to be successful amounts to a considerable knowledge in many different fields. The best philosophy in HCI targets users to devise interaction and interfaces, i.e., "know thy users" (Kim, G.J., 2015, p.4). Ideally, comprehensive information about the target user attributes should be collected and analyzed to determine their skill levels, tendencies, probable preferences, and capabilities (physical and mental). Armed with such information, one can accurately model the interaction and design the most appropriate interface for the target users. Kim, G.J. (2015, p.6) presented another almost-commonsensical principle which is to base HCI design on the understanding of the task. The the job to be accomplished by the user through the use of the interactive system constitutes the task referred to. The task is further simplified by user analysis and interaction modelling. The principle which has a theoretical basis is to design the interaction with as little memory load as possible (Kim, G.J., 2015, p.7). Tasks that require less memory burden, long or short term can easily be carried out by humans. In the longer term, the burden to remove the memory load can be removed by keeping consistency, to (a) both within an application and across different applications, and (b) both the interaction model and interface implementation (Kim, G.J., 2015, p.8).

The practice of interacting with a computing environment developed mainly from the inception of the graphical user interface (GUI) in the early 1980s, where the dominant interaction model was the direct manipulation mode (Corso, J.J., 2005, p.1). Direct manipulation describes the user's ability to effect immediate changes in the computer-state by directly interacting with the application objects through the keyboard, which is in contrast to earlier generations of interfaces that required the user to pre-program the whole session or learn a complex procedural command-language. According to Corso, J.J., 2005, p.1), the direct manipulation model comprises four principles:

1. Physical actions through the movement and selection by input devices.

2. Representation of the objects of interest.

3. Approach to learning.

**4.** Visible operations on the object of interest.

The direct interaction model brought proficiency with the user interface to a broad spectrum of users, and gave rise to the current generation of computer interfaces: the "Windows, Icons, Menus and Pointers" (WIMP) generation, which is the style of interface to which we have become accustomed. Corso, J.J. (2005, p.2) stated that "A post-WIMP interface is that it does not depend on classical 2D widgets such as menus and icons but contains at least one interaction technique. Ultimately it will involve all senses in parallel, natural language communication and multiple users." In this context, it was noted that the interaction evolved into a duplex learning process on a per-user basis, for interaction is, essentially, a means of communication between the human and the computer. It was further observed that humans are highly adaptable and are known to bring a vast amount of domain knowledge from everyday real-world activities. A key enabling technology for the post-WIMP interface is computer vision, which is about giving the computer the ability to see its surroundings and to interpret them. Computer vision holds great promise for effecting a natural and intuitive communication between human and machine. Corso, J.J. (2005, p.ii) investigated the integration of passive, vision-based sensing into large-scale environments and conventional interfaces. The Visual Interaction Cues (VICs) paradigm, a new methodology for vision-based human-computer interaction, was proposed by Corso, J.J. (2005, p.ii). VICs use monocular and stereoscopic video to share the perceptual space between the user and computer. In this space, the interface component is a localized region in the image(s) which nullifies the need to visually track the user and models the interaction as an expected stream of visual cues corresponding to a gesture (Corso, J.J., 2005, p.ii). When the finger moves to press a push-button it generates an interaction cue, just like a 3D hand posture for a communication in sign language.

Advances in mobile technologies and communication infrastructure presents new opportunities for mobile audio input/out mechanisms. New approaches and methods are now needed in HCI to equip researchers with a better understanding of designing interactive systems. There are new interactive possibilities to be explored in audio-based mobile technology. The increasing popularity of smartphones has proved the portability, adaptability and 'always on' capability of geo-locative interactive systems (Chamberlain, A., *et al* , 2017, p.25). For mobile interactions to be cantered around sound, we need to exploit the opportunities in this field and pay particular attention to the possible emotional and subjective values inscribed in the use of sound. Sound recording on mobile devices is a practice with unlimited possibilities in sound propagation and communication. Sound recording in mobile HCI can benefit from autoethnographies.

Office productivity applications have been enhanced through the use of the GUI-based style of interaction between the users and computing devices, thus making them more user-friendly. However, the growing pervasive and ubiquitous nature of computing devices is changing due to the advances in bandwidth and mobility. The modern future trend is to develop natural, intuitive, adaptive, and unobtrusive interfaces. "Perceptive media" combines multimedia display and machine perception in order to create useful, adaptive, responsive interfaces between people and technology (Turk, M., 2018, p.1). According to Turk, M. (2018, p.1), there now are many non-GUI (or "post-WIMP") technologies, such as speech recognition, computer vision, virtual reality, spatial sound , and haptics that promise to change the status quo in computer-human interaction. However, in general, hardware has changed much more dramatically than software, especially software for HCI. Turk, M. (2018, p.2) suggested several alternatives on how human computer interaction can proceed in the future, including the simplification and disappearance of the interface whilst accommodating natural ways of interaction as provided in artificial intelligence.

Computers can be used as a tool for helping blind people, and so can be used as an interface between the person and the environment trying to compensate human vision lack. The idea is to use computer vision within a device which can tell with voice or updating a braille device what is around the person. This can be done with one camera if the device is moveable with the person or with more cameras if thinking about a room or a house where to displace the cameras. Another aid offered by computer vision application can be the development of an interface for deaf people helping them, for example, allowing an easier communication with other people. The idea is making a device capable of recognizing the sign language to allow the consequent using of that information for many scenarios, for example allowing communication with people who doesn't know the sign language. The future relies on the need to develop effective, natural, and transparent methods for HCI. A comprehensive understanding of interaction technologies is required for envisioning, designing, and implementing the user interface. Electrooculography (EOG) and computer-vision-based eye tracking are two of the most promising eye-tracking methods for measurements in daily life settings, making vision-based eye tracking a green field.

HCI is about the design and planning of interaction between humans and computing devices ( Atanasova, D., and Hristova, P., 2011, p.120). Through the past three decades, HCI has successfully integrated the engineering goal of improving the usability of computer systems and applications with its scientific concerns, which constitutes a methodology and a body of technical knowledge. According to Atanasova, D., and Hristova, P. (2011, p.120), HCI professionals should have a better understanding of the factors that determine the nature of interaction between users and computing technology, demonstrate application of the techniques development and tools for the provision of suitable computer systems, and enhance the interaction with the individual and group. A study of HCI helps people with various disabilities and special needs to effectively use computing devices by enhancing technologies accessibility and usability, for example people with cerebral palsy or other severe disabilities. Cerebral palsy hinders a user's mobility and cognitive abilities. HCI further facilitates through hand gestures the development of computer games, control of mechanical systems, interaction with visualization systems and control of consumer electronics.

In summary, HCI bridges the gap between humans and computing devices with respect to observation of interactions, analysis of the involved interactions and the the human consequences of the interaction. The focus of HCI is the practice of usability which includes look-and-feel features, appeal, utility, efficiency, effectiveness and safety.

# 3. INTEGRATIVE CONCLUSION

The paper presented an analytical exposition, critical context and integrative conclusion on the trends and best practices Human Computer Interaction (HCI) and Computer Vision. Information Technology (IT) is essentially an integrated person-machine system that provides information support operations, management and decision-making. The interaction between humans and machines is performed through a user interface, that is a collection of devices that enable the user to manipulate and to monitor the system status. HCI studies the interactions between end users and computers (Erdem, I.A., 2003, p.1). Human Computer Interaction (HCI) focuses on the interactions between human and computer systems to achieve the IT system functionality, user experience, usability, the support of user interaction effectiveness (Draganova, A, and Doran, P., 2013, p.245). HCI is concerned about the usability of the systems. According to Nielsen cited in Erdem (2003, p.1) the five criteria of usability are learnability, efficiency, memorability, errors and satisfaction.

HCI is abound with practical research methods such as field experiments, formal experiments, field studies, surveys, focus groups, interviews, usability tests, contextual inquiry, case studies, ethnography, diary studies, automated data collection, and experience sampling (Lopes, A.G., 2016, p.365). HCI, as a multidisciplinary field, draws benefits and contributions from diverse areas such as psychology, organisational and social science, computer science, and cognitive science, with the view to investigate user experience and interaction with technology. HCI, as a multidisciplinary field, draws benefits and contributions from diverse areas such as psychology, organisational and social science, computer science, and cognitive science, with the view to investigate user experience and interaction with technology.

Surface technology eliminates input/output devices through a touch sensitive feature which plays the role of input/output devices as a result of the merger between the physical and the virtual world (Farooq, U., *et al,* 2011, p.25). Through surface technology, the user eliminates the use of GUI mediums and reduces the gap between the physical and the virtual world. There are two classes of surface technology, one for the display and the other one which uses a touch sensitive mechanism for the interpretation of user signals

The direct interaction model brought proficiency with the user interface to a broad spectrum of users, and gave rise to the current generation of computer interfaces: the "Windows, Icons, Menus and Pointers" (WIMP) generation, which is the style of interface to which we have become accustomed. The best philosophy in HCI targets users to devise interaction and interfaces, i.e., "know thy users" (Kim, G.J., 2015, p.4). Ideally, comprehensive information about the target user attributes should be collected and analyzed to determine their skill levels, tendencies, probable preferences, and capabilities (physical and mental). Kim, G.J. (2015, p.6) presented another almost-commonsensical principle which is to base HCI design on the understanding of the task. User analysis and interaction modelling simplifies our understanding of the task on hand. Designing interaction with as little memory load as possible is a principle that also has a theoretical basis (Kim, G.J., 2015, p.7).

The direct interaction model brought proficiency with the user interface to a broad spectrum of users, and gave rise to the current generation of computer interfaces: the "Windows, Icons, Menus and Pointers" (WIMP) generation, which is the style of interface to which we have become accustomed. The field of human-computer interaction has increasingly become more devoted to the processes and context for the user interface.

# References

ATANASOVA, D., and Hristova, P., (2011). Human Computer Interaction, Proceedings of the Union Scientists - RUSE VOL . 8 / 2011, https://www.researchgate.net/publication/282278596.

CHAMBERLAIN, A., Bodker, M., Hazzard, A., McGookin, D., De Roure, D., Wilcox, P., and Papangelis, K., (2017). Audio Technology and Mobile Human Computer Interaction: From Space and Place, to Social Media, Music, Composition and Creation, International Journal of Mobile Human Computer Interaction, Volume 9, Issue 4, October-December 2017, Copyright © 2017, IGI Global.

CORSO, J.J., (2005). Techniques for vision-based human-computer interaction, Ph.D. Dissertation, The Johns Hopkins University, 2015.

DRAGANOVA, A., and Doran, P., (2013). Use of HCI Components into IT Courses, International Journal of Information and Education Technology, Vol. 3, No. 2, April 2013

ERDEM, I.A., (2003). Vision-based Human-Computer Interaction using Laser Pointer, M.Sc. Thesis, Middle East Technical University, July, 2003.

FAROOQ, U., Iqbal, M.A., and Nazir, S., (2011). A glance into the future of human computer interaction, International Journal of Computer Science, Engineering and Applications (IJCSEA) Vol.1, No.3, June 2011, DOI : 10.5121/ijcsea.2011.1303.

KIM, G.J., (2015). Human-Computer Interaction: Fundamentals and Practice, TCRC Press, Taylor & Francis Group, ISBN 978-1-4822-3389-6, http://www.taylorandfrancis.com, http://www.crcpress.com,

LOPES, A.G., (2016). Using research methods in human computer interaction to design technology for resilience, JISTEM - Journal of Information Systems and Technology Management, Revista de Gestão da Tecnologia e Sistemas de Informação, Vol. 13, No. 3, Set/Dez., 2016 pp. 363-388, ISSN online: 1807-1775, DOI: 10.4301/S1807-17752016000300001.

TURK, M., (2018). Perceptive Media: Machine Perception and Human Computer Interaction, Computer Science Department, University of California Santa Barbara, CA 93106 USA, 2018.

# YOUR KNOWLEDGE HAS VALUE

- We will publish your bachelor's and
  master's thesis, essays and papers

- Your own eBook and book -
  sold worldwide in all relevant shops

- Earn money with each sale

Upload your text at www.GRIN.com
and publish for free